A LifeGuide

COUPLES OF THE
OLD TESTAMENT

9 STUDIES FOR INDIVIDUALS OR GROUPS

Dale & Sandy Larsen

With Notes for Leaders

IVP Connect

An imprint of InterVarsity Press
Downers Grove, Illinois

InterVarsity Press
P.O. Box 1400, Downers Grove, IL 60515-1426
World Wide Web: www.ivpress.com
E-mail: mail@ivpress.com

InterVarsity Press® is the book-publishing division of InterVarsity Christian Fellowship®, a student movement active on campus at hundreds of universities, colleges and schools of nursing in the United States of America, and a member movement of the International Fellowship of Evangelical Students. For information about local and regional activities, write Public Relations Dept., InterVarsity Christian Fellowship, 6400 Schroeder Rd., P.O. Box 7895, Madison, WI 53707-7895, or visit the IVCF website at <www.intervarsity.org>.

LifeGuide® is a registered trademark of InterVarsity Christian Fellowship.

All Scripture quotations, unless otherwise indicated, are taken from the Holy Bible, New International Version®, NIV®. Copyright ©1973, 1978, 1984 by International Bible Society. Used by permission of Zondervan Publishing House. All rights reserved.

Cover photograph: Dennis Flaherty

ISBN-10: 0-8308-3048-0
ISBN-13: 978-0-8308-3048-0

Printed in the United States of America ∞

P	20	19	18	17	16	15	14	13	12
Y	20	19	18	17	16	15			

Contents

Getting the Most Out of
Couples of the Old Testament

Some people say that when couples have been married a long time, they start to look like each other. There may be truth in it. Married couples take on each other's mannerisms, tastes and favorite phrases. They may even take on each other's facial expressions. Or perhaps we see them together so often that when we see one, we automatically see the other.

One college student told us she did not want to get married because she feared she would lose her own identity. We tried to assure her that she would still be herself; yet we knew that in another way she would never again be *only* herself. When a man and woman marry, they become part of one another's lives, for good or harm. Marriage enriches and complicates, restricts and frees couples' lives in ways that could never happen if they were single.

Our young friend's fear is common today. The drive for individual fulfillment puts pressure on even the strongest marriages. In times of conflict, couples get little help from the world around them. The pressures to divide can be stronger than the pressures to stay together. A young single man told us that he gets very nervous when he sees how many of his friends are already divorced. A young married woman pointed out the same phenomenon among her friends, and she said it made her enormously sad.

No wonder some people have decided marriage isn't necessary. They put it on hold indefinitely or skip marriage entirely. Society debates even the legal definition of *marriage*.

If only we could go back to the simplicity of Bible times! Back then family ties were close. Marriage vows were sacred. Men and women lived under the lordship of God himself. They even heard from God directly—no wondering about the choice of a marriage partner; just ask the Lord. Married life was easier then.

Or was it? Look at some of the couples in Scripture, and you will find marriages as complex and full of difficulty as any we can find today.

In the pages of the Old Testament there are couples who live with chronic disappointment and couples who overcome all obstacles to be together. There are in-laws who can't stand each other and in-laws who can't bear to be apart. There's a husband who thinks he is marrying one woman and actually marries another. There's a wife who risks death if she walks in on her husband unannounced. There's a husband who takes back his wife when she becomes a prostitute. There are arranged marriages, fiercely loving marriages, enduring marriages, an instant marriage, a coerced marriage and even a couple who had the perfect marriage—and blew it!

In these strange but timeless stories (and some of them are *very* strange to our culture!) we have much to learn about marriage, God and ourselves. These were flawed women and men who had a great God and who loved each other, and all of us can find commonality in that. After all, like the people of the Bible, most of us marry and most of us are glad we did. Like the people of the Bible, we are happier if we live out our marriage vows—and all the rest of life—under the guidance and love of God.

The principles we learn from these biblical couples ultimately apply to all of us, married or single. While this LifeGuide study is a natural fit for a couples Bible study, it is useful for any Bible study group or for individuals in personal study.

Each session begins with questions for group discussion and personal reflection. At the close of each session is a "Now or Later" section, which provides ideas for further study and application. Each "Now or Later" section includes an activity for couples.

May the Lord help you find connection with these couples from history and use their lives to touch your own life, no matter what your marital status or situation.

Suggestions for Individual Study

1. As you begin each study, pray that God will speak to you through his Word.

2. Read the introduction to the study and respond to the personal reflection question or exercise. This is designed to help you focus on God and on the theme of the study.

3. Each study deals with a particular passage—so that you can delve into the author's meaning in that context. Read and reread the passage to be studied. The questions are written using the language of the New International Version, so you may wish to use that version of the Bible. The New Revised Standard Version is also recommended.

4. This is an inductive Bible study, designed to help you discover for yourself what Scripture is saying. The study includes three types of questions. *Observation* questions ask about the basic facts: who, what, when, where and how. *Interpretation* questions delve into the meaning of the passage. *Application* questions help you discover the implications of the text for growing in Christ. These three keys unlock the treasures of Scripture.

Write your answers to the questions in the spaces provided or in a personal journal. Writing can bring clarity and deeper understanding of yourself and of God's Word.

5. It might be good to have a Bible dictionary handy. Use it to look up any unfamiliar words, names or places.

6. Use the prayer suggestion to guide you in thanking God for what you have learned and to pray about the applications that have come to mind.

7. You may want to go on to the suggestion under "Now or Later," or you may want to use that idea for your next study.

Suggestions for Members of a Group Study

1. Come to the study prepared. Follow the suggestions for individual study mentioned above. You will find that careful preparation will greatly enrich your time spent in group discussion.

2. Be willing to participate in the discussion. The leader of your group will not be lecturing. Instead, he or she will be encouraging the members of the group to discuss what they have learned. The leader will be asking the questions that are found in this guide.

3. Stick to the topic being discussed. Your answers should be based on the verses which are the focus of the discussion and not on outside authorities such as commentaries or speakers. These studies focus on a particular passage of Scripture. Only rarely should you refer to other portions of the Bible. This allows for everyone to participate in indepth study on equal ground.

4. Be sensitive to the other members of the group. Listen attentively when they describe what they have learned. You may be surprised by their insights! Each question assumes a variety of answers. Many questions do not have "right" answers, particularly questions that aim at meaning or application. Instead the questions push us to explore the passage more thoroughly.

When possible, link what you say to the comments of others. Also, be affirming whenever you can. This will encourage some of the more hesitant members of the group to participate.

5. Be careful not to dominate the discussion. We are sometimes so eager to express our thoughts that we leave too little opportunity for others to respond. By all means participate! But allow others to also.

6. Expect God to teach you through the passage being discussed and through the other members of the group. Pray that you will have an enjoyable and profitable time together, but also that as a result of the study you will find ways that you can take action individually and/or as a group.

7. Remember that anything said in the group is considered confidential and should not be discussed outside the group unless specific permission is given to do so.

8. If you are the group leader, you will find additional suggestions at the back of the guide.

1

Adam and Eve

Ideal Companions

Genesis 2:15—3:13

With the possible exception of Noah's ark, the story of Adam and Eve has been the subject of more cartoons and comedy routines than any other story in the Bible. The tree, the forbidden fruit (always an apple), the serpent, the fig leaves—all the stereotypical images pop into our minds when we think "Adam and Eve."

The jokes amuse us; but if we want to learn from God through the lives of the first couple, we must disregard parodies and take a thoughtful look at the Scripture. We need to enter the story *before* the Fall. Adam and Eve show us God's original, ideal plan for human marriage. They also demonstrate how sin has distorted relationships between all men and women.

GROUP DISCUSSION. What advantages and disadvantages would there be to being the first man and woman on the face of the earth?

PERSONAL REFLECTION. How have you seen God's love operating in and through your marriage? (If you are single, what do you think makes an ideal marriage?)

We are about to enter the Genesis story shortly after God created the heavens and the earth and made the first man. Chapter two tells us that God planted a lush garden "in the east, in Eden" (v. 8). *Read Genesis 2:15-25.*

---

1. Throughout this passage, how does God show his love and care for the first humans through his provision of meaningful work?

guidance? Spoke to Adam and told he all this exapt the tree of Good & Evil

companionship? Anamilo than Eve (woman from man)

How has God shown his love and care for you in similar ways?

He has always Be there with me in the Holy Spirit. And he on earth given me a wonderful Husband.

2. What freedoms and what limitations did God give the man (2:15-17)? The whole Garden was His Eat Freely!

(ExcEpt the tree of Knowledge of good & eu

3. Even in the perfection of Eden, there was one thing that was "not good"—for the man to be alone (2:18). What does that say to you about essential human nature? I will make a helper Just right for him.

(We need other People)

4. If you had been Adam, meeting the parade of animals God brought to you (2:19-20), what emotions might you have experienced?

Over welmend at a wonderful gift worthy and honored to name them. Blowed away.

5. What significance do you find in the woman being created from one of the man's ribs (2:21-22)?

He took from the man not durt. Took most all the feman side of him from the man and made a woman. (She took his breath away)

6. Genesis 2:23-25 obviously describes a relationship of physical intimacy between Adam and Eve. In addition, what other sorts of intimacy are implied? *ClosNess (Like we have from God. can be Free, Enjoy, Helpmate.*

7. To what extent do you think this sort of closeness is possible for a husband and wife today? *Very much if they Both have God as the center of there own life and of them together.*

If Adam and Eve's relationship seems too good to last, that is because we see it from this side of the Fall. God meant it to last forever. Sadly, it did not, and all creation still feels the effects. *Read Genesis 3:1-13.*

8. The apostle Paul wrote that Eve was "deceived by the serpent's cunning" (2 Corinthians 11:3). What deceptive strategies did the serpent use to tempt Eve to sin against God (3:1-5)? *He (?) What God/Adam Spoke to her. woman Said (or Even touch it) God Never Said that. Telling her it was ok and making her want to know more and(?) why would God hold.*

9. What responsibility for their sin does Eve bear, and what responsibility does Adam bear for their sin (3:6)? *this back if I could be more like m...*

They Both (Full responsibil) God Spoke to Both of them. Says Adam was beside he when She took a bit and then he took ne. He could have hit it out of her hand and said No Eve (we obey God

10. How did eating the forbidden fruit change the way Adam and Eve responded to each other and to God (3:7-13)? *Eyes opened and felt new things like Shame, They Felt Deviued from God. Not worth Being in front of God After what they did. They wanted to cover up themaself! There si...*

11. What are some issues for which wives and husbands typically blame one another? *Miscomaction, Not listening to each other.*

12. If you are married, what is an area in which you typically try to sidestep responsibility and accuse your spouse? *House work oh Babe I told we 3 times.*

If you are single, where do you typically try to avoid responsibility by blaming the people closest to you?

13. What changes will you make in order to take responsibility for a specific fault? *To Speak in a louing way and Be more of a helpmate to my husband*

Pray that marriages—your own and those of people you care about—will have honesty and intimacy in every sense of the word.

Now or Later

CONSIDER: humanity's first sin was not the end of the story. Christians have historically seen in Genesis 3:15 the first prophecy of the coming Redeemer, Jesus Christ. In a set time limit, list as many of your own mistakes, sins and oversights as possible. Then, for each one, meditate on how Christ has forgiven it and even used it for good.

THINK of a couple who exemplifies Christian marriage for you. Write a note to that couple (or, if one is not living, to the surviving spouse) to express your appreciation for their example. Mention specific qualities you have seen in their marriage. Recall a specific event where their love for each other and for God shone through. If both people are deceased, write the letter anyway and use it to thank God for the lives of those two people.

FOR COUPLES. Adam and Eve are the only couple in history who could look at each other and honestly say "You're perfect." And even that didn't last long! Take time to tell each other what you most value and appreciate about each other. Then admit that you know you are not perfect and that you accept that the other person is not perfect. Thank God for the gift of each other.

2

Abraham and Sarah

Waiting Together

Genesis 17:1-8, 15-22; 21:1-7

A wedding is a celebration of hope. Many couples marry young when endless years of happiness seem to stretch before them. They have high expectations of their life together. They are sure they will be happy because all their dreams will come true.

Life seldom fulfills all our youthful hopes. Sometimes a couple's plans get put on hold and they have to wait . . . and wait. What seemed an eternity of happiness unfolds into an eternity of "not yet." Whether the wait is for children, for stable employment, for a home of their own or for family members to find faith in Christ, they must wait in the strength and grace of God.

GROUP DISCUSSION. How important to a marriage is patience, and why?

PERSONAL REFLECTION. When has waiting been most difficult for you? When has it been most rewarding?

God promised Abram that he would become a great nation (Genesis 12:2). Abram complained that he was childless and that a household servant would be his heir, but God answered that Abram's descendants would be like the stars (Genesis 15:2-3). Faith faltered, and at the urging of his wife Sarai, Abram took Sarai's maidservant Hagar and fathered a son by her, Ishmael (Genesis 16). Thirteen years later, and twenty-four years after the initial promise, God appeared to Abram to confirm his message of hope. *Read Genesis 17:1-8, 15-22.*

---

1. Imagine Abram, age ninety-nine, as he listens to God's progression of promises in 17:1-8. How do you think he responds to each on the following scale of belief?

| Unquestioning certainty | Hope against hope | Some misgivings | Sounds too good to be true | Incredulity |

What would be your reaction(s)?

I have to see it to Believe it.

---

2. God's words were not only for Abraham. What specific promises did God make to Sarah (17:15-19)?

Name Change, a son, Mother of many Nations things will Come forth.

3. Notice the different names that are given throughout this passage (17:1, 5, 15, 19). What is the significance of names in this passage?

God gave it to them.

---

4. Even in the presence of God, Abraham could not hold back his laughter at the thought that he and Sarah would have a child (17:17). Why does Abraham's suggestion in 17:18 seem more reasonable than what God has promised to do?

Enjoy the blessing

---

5. When have you thought that your solution to a problem was more realistic than God's? *When you can't see the full picture and you think the here and now are better.*

6. Why does God's answer (17:19-22) demand faith on the part of both Abraham and Sarah?

BC they had to wait

7. When a couple's life does not go as hoped and planned, how can they help and encourage each other to trust God? *By this truth.*

Much happened in the next year of Abraham and Sarah's life. The covenant sign of circumcision was initiated. The couple received three heavenly visitors who repeated the promise that Sarah would have a son. Sodom and Gomorrah were destroyed. Abraham moved his household into the Negev. Then, at last, their years of waiting were rewarded. *Read Genesis 21:1-7.* *Sarah had Isaac a baby boy.*

8. As God finally gives Sarah and Abraham a son of their own, how does 21:1-2 express his special love and concern for them?

Did everything he Promised.

9. What do Abraham's actions in 21:3-5 reveal about his attitude toward the God who had answered his prayers? *Abram did what God asked.*

10. How would you compare Sarah's laughter in 21:6-7 *(cleabrting)* with Abraham's laughter in 17:17? *(unbelief)*

11. If you know someone who is waiting on God, how will you encourage that person this week? *To Pray for and with them. Send God's word of truth and Promies. How Faithful God is.*

12. What areas of your life will you surrender to God's timing?

- Have a baby boy myself
- Our Disness that is 100% His
- my life & family.

Pray that you will wait for the Lord's answers to your problems and prayers. Ask especially that you will be restrained from charging ahead of God. Pray that husbands and wives will encourage each other in times when impatience leads to tension between them.

Now or Later

THINK of something for which you are now in a time of waiting. Write out your thoughts about it in a letter to the Lord. Tell him honestly

- how you feel about the wait
- what you have learned about him through the experience
- what you have learned about yourself during this time
- what unanswered questions you still have

If appropriate, share the letters in your group. If your letter is very long, in consideration of others, read only an excerpt.

Keep your letter in a place you can find it again. Commit yourself to rereading it periodically, and promise to re-read it when you see your answer from the Lord.

LOOK at Galatians 4:21-31, in which Paul uses the son "born in the ordinary way" and the son "born as the result of a promise" to draw a parallel between God's old and new covenants (the Law and Christ).

FOR COUPLES. Choose an area in which the two of you have had to wait on the Lord. It may be an existing situation or one you have already weathered together. Think and make notes about these questions:

- How has waiting on the Lord deepened your regard for each other?
- What has the wait taught you about the Lord?

Share your responses with each other; talk and pray about them together.

3

Isaac and Rebekah

How God Makes a Match

Genesis 24:26-67

"Wait until you hear how we met. You'll never believe it." Have you heard a husband or wife say that? Maybe you have said it about your own marriage. No matter how unusual your story, it can hardly match the story of Isaac and Rebekah, who got married as soon as they saw each other.

Outlandish as it sounds to us today, Isaac and Rebekah's meeting was not so unusual for that time and culture. The most important factor remains timeless: God works through circumstances and brings marriage partners together if they submit to his will and wait for his choice.

GROUP DISCUSSION. Recall some stories about how married couples met. What is the most unusual story you have heard? (It may be your own!)

PERSONAL REFLECTION. If you are married, how do you see the Lord's hand in bringing the two of you together? If you are single, how do you believe you can know whether a particular person is God's choice for you? → Felt it in my spirit.

In study 2 you read about Isaac, the child of promise. When Isaac grew up, his father Abraham did not want him to marry one of the local Canaanite women. Abraham preferred someone from back in his own

#58 They aske if her she was willing to go.

home area, along what is now the border between Turkey and Syria. (Isaac's mother Sarah had died some years earlier.) Too old to make the journey, Abraham sent his most trusted servant to find a wife for Isaac. In answer to the servant's prayers, God led him to meet Rebekah, the granddaughter of Abraham's brother. *Read Genesis 24:26-67.*

1. Throughout this story, how do you see God's sovereignty in action?

lined up with everything the Lord told The servent.(a Place to stay the young woman

What recent example (large or small) can you give of God's sovereignty at work in some area of your life? *When you let go and allow God to have it all.*

2. Consider the servant's response to meeting Rebekah (vv. 26-27). What do his words and actions reveal about the character of this man whom Abraham sent to find a wife for Isaac? *Faithful, Bold, trustworthy,*

3. The servant had just finished a journey of over four hundred miles by camel caravan. Certainly he would want to eat and rest. How do you explain his urgency to get to the matter at hand (vv. 28-33)? *He did not want to keep His master waiting. He had a watchful eye out for the bride to be.*

4. When and how did you realize the importance of finding God's choice of a marriage partner? *When I felt in my Spirit that this is the man I could be free with and not hide things oe who I was. that He was God Set I Just needed trust the one*

5. Rebekah had met the servant and his retinue at the well; she had *who Sent Him.*

accepted costly jewelry from him (v. 22), no doubt with an idea of what it meant; but she had not heard his story. Imagine her now as she hears him explain his mission (vv. 34-49). What would be her apprehensions?

her hopes? *To be the right one for his mission. That God chose her.*

6. Abraham was the first in his family to believe in the Lord, and he left his father's household shortly afterward (Genesis 12:1-4). Rebekah may not have known of the Lord. Her brother Laban possessed images that were "household gods" (Genesis 31:19). As Rebekah listened to the servant's story, what would she learn about the Lord?

That he is faithful and Just.

7. What role does Rebekah's own willingness play in the story (vv. 50-61)? *#58*

They ask if she wanted to go. She was not forced.

8. When Rebekah set out to marry Isaac, she was accompanied by servants and by her nurse who had taken care of her in childhood (vv. 59-61). When we marry, we still maintain ties to our earlier lives. How is a marriage affected by a partner's attitude toward those ties?

9. Isaac does not appear in the story until verse 62. From verses 62-67 what do you discern about what was going through his heart all this time? *Who is this beauty you have blessed me with Lord. I will honor you and my parents.*

10. If you are married, what difference will it make in your marriage if you have complete confidence that the Lord has brought the two of you together? *You lean on God more You dont ever think is ths the right one.*

If you are single, how can you more fully submit your future to the will and wisdom of God? *Don't Put married as a Idol Be Faith to all God has Called you to be do.*

11. How will you honor God's wisdom and sovereignty in the choice of marriage partners in your own marriage (or singleness)? *To Remembaber CK is Gods 1st and a blessing and help mate.*

in other marriages?

Pray that Christians who are single will submit to God's loving choice for them, whether in a future marriage partner or in continuing singleness. Pray that Christian couples will live in the glad assurance that the Lord has picked them out for each other.

Now or Later

DISCUSS how the Lord's hand can be evident in bringing even non-Christian couples together. Use examples from your own knowledge, or use the following stories:

- Two people, neither of them Christians, meet in college and marry after they graduate. They move to another city for work. They are successful in their careers, but they have trouble meeting people and making friends. Then a neighbor in their apartment building invites them to church, where they find themselves socializing with mostly Christian couples.

- A young woman experiments with various spiritual paths, none of them Christian. Her pattern is to follow an intriguing philosophy for a while and then drop it to take up something new. Along the way she meets a young man with a similar history. They fall in love but have no long-term commitment to each other. One day, out of curiosity, the man buys a Bible in a used bookstore. The woman at first ridicules his interest but then begins to dip into the book for herself. As they tentatively discuss what they have read, they feel discontented with the spiritual paths they have taken, but they aren't sure what to do next.

REFLECT: although Christians are warned not to marry unbelievers (2 Cor 6:14), many find themselves in that situation. One partner may become a Christian after marriage. Or a Christian may marry without realizing the importance of a shared faith. In either case the believer will be tempted to have second thoughts about the marriage. Study Paul's teaching on unequal marriages in 1 Corinthians 7:12-16 and 2 Corinthians 6:14—7:1.

FOR COUPLES. Recall again the story of how you met. If you can't remember (or agree!), or if you have known each other all your lives, recall other significant steps in your relationship. Perhaps you can remember the first time you realized you were God's choice for each other. (You may have realized it at different times!) Thank the Lord for how he brought you together and for how he daily sustains your relationship. Resolve to rely on him to keep your marriage strong. Put up or identify some particular object in your home to remind you of your resolve—and of his faithfulness that makes your resolve possible.

4

Jacob and Rachel

Love Endures

Genesis 29:1-30

Has your love life sometimes resembled a soap opera? Even if it has, you would probably not want to trade places with Jacob, one of the sons of Isaac and Rebekah.

In study 2 we read about Rebekah and Isaac's arranged marriage. They loved each other, and God granted them prosperity and twin sons, Jacob and Esau. However, Isaac favored Esau, while Rebekah favored Jacob, and favoritism soon caused problems. When the boys grew up, Rebekah urged Isaac to send Jacob away to find a wife from her own people. Her motive was not so much to avoid the local women as to save Jacob's life. Esau was plotting to kill Jacob for cheating him out of his birthright and blessing (Genesis 25:27-34; 27:1-46).

What a way to set out to find a marriage partner! Jacob headed for the home of Laban, his mother's brother. It must have started out as a desperate and fearful journey, but on the way the Lord met Jacob and promised him great blessings. Jacob vowed (although conditionally) to serve the Lord (Genesis 28:10-22).

GROUP DISCUSSION. Do people find it easy or difficult to trick you? Give some examples (if they will not embarrass you or someone else).

PERSONAL REFLECTION. When have you been tricked by someone—
not a harmless prank but a hurtful deception? How did you deal with
the situation and with the defrauder?

Armed with God's promises—and a natural determination to get what
he could out of life—Jacob arrived at his uncle's home. *Read Genesis
29:1-30.*

1. Consider the various motivations of the main characters in this
story: Jacob, Rachel, Leah and Laban. Which of these do you identify
with and why?

Jacob, To wait on God to open the door

2. In verses 1-14 how do Jacob, Rachel and Laban all appear to have
favorable prospects?

To work 7 years for Rachel

3. What is the role of hope in marriage (generally)?

That it will be well a positive Outcome.

What is its role in Christian marriage? *To be Christ Center*

hot in Christ to forfill in our marriage.

4. Consider Jacob's bargain with Laban (vv. 15-20). What does it tell
you about Rachel's worth in Jacob's eyes? *Rachel is*

*worth not Just 7yr But total
of 14year all bc se was brearth
taken and he de*

(PS:37:4)

Hope That He Knows and our faith to Fulfill.

5. What are some ways couples can show how highly they value each other?

By the way they talk to each other
By how they act together.

6. How and why did Laban play havoc with Jacob and Rachel's hopes (vv. 21-26)? *Bc, He Followed Cosdoms to marriage the oldest 1st.*

7. When Jacob discovered the deception, what do you think were his possible choices of action? *To get mad and give Leah back to Laban.*

8. Which did he choose and why (vv. 27-30)? *To wait till a week and and Jacob agreed to work another 7yre For Rachel.*

9. Even in the face of Laban's deception, God worked out a way for Jacob and Rachel to be together. When has God overcome an obstacle in your marriage (or in some other important relationship)? *with CK and I to Be together*

10. This story is full of imperfect people, but the Lord cared enough to meet their needs for love. Where do you need to trust the Lord to meet your needs?

- with me changing and Growing.
- my Kids
- my husband.

11. How can you encourage the hopes of a couple facing difficult times? *In Prayer, This Story.*

Pray that marriages will be filled with the hope that arises from trust in God.

Now or Later

MEDITATE on the words of the Song of Songs (or Song of Solomon):

> Many waters cannot quench love;
>   rivers cannot wash it away.
> If one were to give
>   all the wealth of his house for love,
>   it would be utterly scorned.
>   (Song of Songs 8:7)

How do these words express the love of Rachel and Jacob?

FOR COUPLES. Read the above passage from the Song of Songs. Identify some of the "many rivers" which have threatened your relationship. Recall how the Lord has brought you through them. Thank him that your love has endured, and thank him especially for his unquenchable love for you.

5

Boaz and Ruth

Faithfulness Rewarded

Ruth 2:1-13; 4:1-17

Do you get tired of "in-law" jokes? Or do you secretly (or not so secretly) enjoy them? With families so mobile today, many people seldom see their in-laws. Others live near each other and get along well, or perhaps not so well. When we lived in Ukraine, where three and even four generations commonly share one apartment, people asked us why Americans get married and move away from their parents. "Who takes care of the children?" they wondered.

GROUP DISCUSSION. What unique blessings and difficulties have you discovered in in-law relationships?

PERSONAL REFLECTION. Do you believe that God rewards our obedience? Think of possible examples from your own life or the lives of others.

Ruth and Naomi may have the best in-law relationship on record! But the story of Ruth is more than a picture of in-law harmony. It is a story of faithfulness during an unfaithful time in Israel's history.

During the unstable time of the Judges, famine struck the area around Bethlehem. A family of four left to find a better life in Moab. Tragedy followed. Death took the males of the family, until the only people left were the wife Naomi and her two Moabite daughters-in-law, one of whom was Ruth. Naomi decided to return to Bethlehem. She urged her daughters-in-law to stay and find other husbands, but Ruth remained loyal to her in the well-known words, "Your people will be my people and your God my God" (Ruth 1:16). *Read Ruth 2:1-13.*

---

1. Where do you see evidence of Ruth's promise to Naomi that "your people will be my people and your God my God"?

---

2. How did the Lord use Ruth's initiative to bring her and Boaz together (2:1-7)?

---

3. Suppose a single person is expressing frustration that God has not provided a marriage partner. How would you discern whether the person is finding a balance between taking initiative and waiting on God?

---

4. What do you know about the personality of Boaz from 2:4-12?

---

5. Identify what you know about the personality of Ruth from 2:6-13.

6. What does Boaz ask God to do for Ruth, and why (2:12)?

---

7. How does Boaz's prayer serve as a model for how husbands and wives can pray for each other?

For the next several weeks, through the wheat and barley harvests, Ruth worked in the fields (2:23). Naomi wanted to find a husband for Ruth. What better prospect than Boaz? Naomi believed that as Elimelech's kinsman, Boaz had the right to claim Ruth as his wife (though in fact there was a closer relative—3:12). Ruth approached Boaz with what amounted to a proposal of marriage (chapter 3). *Read Ruth 4:1-17.*

---

8. What obstacle stood in the way of Boaz and Ruth marrying (4:1-5)?

---

9. How does Boaz's solution to the problem demonstrate his concern for fairness (4:1-10)?

---

10. The witnesses in the Bethlehem gate pronounced a blessing on Ruth and Boaz (4:11-12). In what ways were both Ruth and Boaz rewarded for their commitment to God and to each other (4:13-17)?

---

11. If you are married, how has the Lord blessed your marriage as a result of your faithfulness to him and to each other?

If you are single, how has the Lord rewarded your faithfulness to him?

---

12. Where do you think you should obey God more fully?

What will you do differently this week as a result?

Thank the Lord for the blessings that come when we follow him. Pray that husbands and wives will be a continual blessing to each other.

Now or Later

COUNT YOUR BLESSINGS. In a set time limit, write all the good things (material or spiritual) that God has given you. Read them over, and thank him for each one. Since the experience has probably oiled up your gratitude, do the exercise again, perhaps with a longer time limit. As an alternative for a group, simultaneously call out as many blessings from God as you can think of in a set time.

FOR COUPLES. Write a letter of gratitude to your spouse. Include your gratitude to God for the blessings that person brings you. Once you have a good start on the letter, put it in a place you can find it easily, or carry it with you. As you think of new reasons to be thankful, add them to your letter. After a set amount of time, exchange letters. As an alternative, leave your letter where your spouse will be surprised to find it. Caution: Don't use the comparative lengths of the two letters to judge each other's hearts. One person may find complimentary words easy to come by, while for the other, even a short note of thanks is an accomplishment.

6

Elkanah and Hannah

Dealing with Disappointment

1 Samuel 1

"Get over it." "Buck up." "Look on the bright side." "It could be worse." People repeat these phrases to us when we're discouraged. Sometimes the words only make us feel worse, but sometimes they are exactly what we need to push us out of immobility.

For the would-be comforter, the situation is awkward. Nobody wants to say the wrong thing. Sometimes it seems there is no right thing to say. At those times "Trust God" may sound too easy, a cliché; but "Trust God" is what we need to hear and what we must do if we want to prevail over disappointment.

GROUP DISCUSSION. How do you usually deal with disappointment? How would you like to handle it differently?

PERSONAL REFLECTION. How do you pray (or how have you prayed) about your disappointments?

Like the story of Ruth, the first part of 1 Samuel takes place in the time of the judges when there was no king in Israel. Jerusalem was not yet the center of worship. The tabernacle which the Israelites had carried in the exodus was set up at Shiloh (Joshua 18:1). *Read 1 Samuel 1.*

1. What qualities marked the relationship between Hannah and Elkanah?

She was his wife

2. What do you think are the best ways for husbands and wives to help each other through disappointments?

Focus on good and encourage each oth thou
it. C

3. Based on your studies so far, what is one possible reason that Elkanah had two wives (vv. 1-2)?

Hannah Could not have a baby

4. How did Elkanah show Hannah that, even though she was childless, he did not disparage her (vv. 3-5)?

We know he loves her and wants to be
en ouh

5. Consider Elkanah's words of comfort in verse 8. If you were Hannah, would you find his words helpful or not, and why?

Self Loss and Put God 1st

6. What does Hannah's prayer tell you about her inner character (vv. 9-16)?

Went with hope.

7. How did Hannah interpret Eli's blessing (vv. 17-18)?

8. Why does it take an extra measure of faith to trust God in the midst of disappointment?

Bc of Sin / Stepping out and being faithful and walking into it.

9. Once God answers our prayers, it is all too easy to take his gifts for granted and neglect to thank him. How did Elkanah and Hannah honor the Lord after the birth of Samuel (vv. 19-28)?

_____

10. Think of some blessings that you take for granted or for which you forget to thank the Lord. How can you express your gratitude to him?

_____

11. What disappointments can you bring to the Lord as Hannah did?

_____

12. Think of someone close to you (your spouse or another person) who has an unrealized dream. What can you do to support and encourage that person?

Place before the Lord all your unrealized plans and frustrated hopes. Ask for a heart that will accept his answer and will remember to be grateful.

Now or Later
STUDY Hannah's song of praise in 1 Samuel 2:1-10. What are the main features of her prayer? Why do you think her prayer makes no men-

tion of Samuel or her previous childlessness? ("She who was barren" in verse 5 cannot be Hannah, because she had borne only Samuel at this time.)

FOR COUPLES. Some couples are very sensitive to each other's unrealized hopes. Others leave their hopes unexpressed, either because each partner thinks the other should automatically know or because a partner prefers to hide old dreams. We do not want to blame our spouses for unrealized hopes, and some youthful schemes do become impractical when we marry. Together take time to thank the Lord for the dreams that he *has* fulfilled for you, even beyond your imaginings. Praise him for the unexpected blessings which neither of you even imagined. Then ask each other if there are ways you can support each other in disappointments. Your responses to question 2 should give guidance.

7

David and Abigail

Wise Intervention

1 Samuel 25:14-42

Recently a college student told us, "My friend was getting married, and I didn't feel right about it. I thought he was making a mistake. Some of his other friends thought so too. But we didn't say anything to him. How do you tell somebody he shouldn't marry that person?"

How do you intervene—*should* you intervene—when you see someone on the wrong path? Husbands and wives, in theory closest to one another, may find it hardest to tell each other the truth. God often calls us to take the risk and step in and say what needs to be said. In the case of David and Abigail, her wise intervention led not only to the rescue of many lives but to their marrying each other!

GROUP DISCUSSION. When has God sent someone wise to intervene in your life? Describe what happened.

PERSONAL REFLECTION. Are you open to listening to wise counsel from others? What benefits do you see, and what cautions do you have?

Hannah and Elkanah's son Samuel grew up to be both judge and prophet for Israel. When Israel demanded a king, God permitted Samuel to anoint Saul as king (1 Samuel 8); but Saul failed as a spiritual leader. Samuel anointed David as Saul's successor-in-waiting (1 Samuel 16:1-13). For years David and his band of followers lived in the wilderness to elude Saul's jealous wrath. After the death of Samuel, David and his men encamped near the flocks of a wealthy man named Nabal, whose wife was Abigail. At shearing time David sent to ask Nabal for payment for guarding his flocks. Nabal rudely refused, and David was furious (1 Samuel 25:1-13). *Read 1 Samuel 25:14-35.*

1. What similarities and what differences do you find between the characters of Abigail and David?

2. Regardless of your gender, would you say your reactions to conflict are more like David's or more like Abigail's? Why?

3. Why did David feel justified in taking revenge on Nabal (vv. 14-22)?

4. How did Abigail show wisdom in the preparation of her defenses (vv. 18-19)?

5. What is the spirit of Abigail's appeal to David (vv. 23-30)?

6. If you had been David listening to Abigail's plea, what range of emotions would you have felt?

7. If you are married, has your spouse ever pacified your anger as Abigail did for David? (If you are single, has anyone else ever done this for you?) What was the outcome?

8. How did David show godliness in his response to Abigail's appeal (vv. 32-35)?

9. Read 1 Samuel 25:36-42. God dealt with Nabal without David's assistance (vv. 36-40). What happened, and how did it confirm what Abigail had told David?

10. When David married Abigail (vv. 40-42) he knew she was a mediator who would urge him to think twice and cool off before he acted impulsively. Why is peacemaking a valuable skill in a marriage?

11. What qualities do you think it takes for a person to be willing to listen to advice?

Which of those qualities do you need to work on in yourself?

Thank God for the people he sends into our lives at exactly the right time. Pray that husbands and wives will listen to each other's wisdom and submit to the voice of God in each other. Pray also that the whole body of Christ will listen to one another and heed each other's wise counsel.

Now or Later

CONSIDER: God might have used this study to prompt you to consider wisely and lovingly intervening in someone's life. If so, pray that God will further confirm that in you and show you if you are to take action.

STUDY Acts 16:6-10. In this passage from the history of the early church, the Holy Spirit twice stops Paul and his companions from going where they intend to go. Then God sends guidance through a vision which is an appeal for help. What are the similarities of this situation with that of David and Abigail? What are the differences?

FOR COUPLES. Recall occasions when your spouse has given you wise advice, even if at the time you did not want to hear it. Identify the times specifically, and thank your spouse for saying the right thing even if it was difficult. Together, thank God for each other's particular gifts of wisdom and insight.

8

Hosea and Gomer

Unconditional Love

Hosea 1 and 3

"I can't forgive her." "I'll never forgive him." We say it and mean it. Then, when we aren't looking, God's love sneaks up on our hearts. Something within us changes. We begin to regard the offender a little differently. The sinner's faults are real, but we see beyond them and get a glimpse of the person's pain. And we start to feel that maybe forgiveness is possible.

GROUP DISCUSSION. What do you think it means to love someone unconditionally?

PERSONAL REFLECTION. What sins (in others) do you find hardest to forgive, and why?

In the Bible there is no marriage more painful—or stranger—than that of Hosea and Gomer. Certainly there is no marriage where forgiveness was less deserved or more generously given. The prophet Hosea spoke for the Lord during the eighth century B.C., a chaotic period in the history of Israel and Judah. Israel, the Northern Kingdom, was in a downward slide which would end in their conquest by Assyria. In the southern kingdom of Judah, a succession of incompetent kings led the people deeper into idolatry. Even the best kings fell into arrogance and pride, and the worst sacrificed his own children to Canaanite gods. The leaders put their futile hopes in foreign alliances, "now calling to Egypt, now turning to Assyria" (Hosea 7:11). In the eyes of the Lord, their idolatry was spiritual adultery. *Read Hosea 1.*

1. What surprising and even shocking elements do you find in this account?

2. For you, what is the most difficult part of this story, and why?

3. What reason did the Lord give Hosea for his command to marry an adulterous woman (1:1-3)?

4. What is the significance of the names of Gomer's children (1:4-9)?

5. Consider the pain Hosea must have experienced with every new infidelity on Gomer's part. To what extent have you considered the pain that your sin causes the Lord?

6. After severe words of judgment, what hope does the Lord offer his people (1:10-11)?

7. What means has God used to show you that he remains faithful to you, even when you have been unfaithful to him?

8. *Read Hosea 3.* How does this next stage in Hosea and Gomer's marriage picture the relationship of God with his people?

9. What internal obstacles would Hosea have had to overcome in order to take Gomer back (3:1)?

10. Hosea "bought" Gomer for a high price (3:2). What are some of the costs of forgiveness (besides financial)?

11. Although Hosea showed unconditional love for Gomer, he put certain restrictions on their reunion. What were they, and why would they have been helpful (3:3)?

12. How do you think Hosea's love might have eventually affected Gomer?

13. At one time or another each of us has been deeply hurt by someone else's sin, whether a spouse or another person. With the power of God to help you, who do you need to offer forgiveness?

Hosea paid a high price to continually forgive Gomer. For our forgiveness God paid the ultimate price—the life of his Son. Thank him for his sacrifice and for not giving up on us.

Now or Later

STUDY Hosea 2. This is a poetic picture of the Lord's judgment on Israel's spiritual adultery, followed by his loving restoration. Here God changes the symbolic names of Gomer's children to reflect his reconciliation with Israel.

FOR COUPLES. Even in the best and closest marriages, couples must often forgive each other. In fact their mutual forgiveness brings them closer together because it prevents roots of bitterness from taking hold (Heb 12:15). Privately identify something in which your spouse has offended you. It may be a trivial matter which you have been chewing on for a long time, or it may be a major sin. Praying for the Lord's strength and help, forgive your spouse with as much of your heart and mind as you can. Tell your spouse that you forgive him or her. Decide beforehand that you will not demand that your spouse say "I forgive you too," because your spouse's forgiveness must also be freely given.

9

King Xerxes and Esther
Courageous Influence

Esther 4:1—5:8

"I can't think of anybody I've ever influenced." A participant in a Bible study said that and apparently believed it. No one else in the group believed it because it is just about impossible *not* to influence the people around us, whether for bad or good. Our circumstances put us in contact with various circles of people. Some we enjoy more than others, but each is an opportunity to positively affect others.

GROUP DISCUSSION. Who has influenced you the most? How did it happen?

PERSONAL REFLECTION. How would you like to be a better influence on other people?

Esther's sphere of influence was forced on her. When Jerusalem fell to the Babylonians in 586 B.C., most of its inhabitants were taken into exile in Babylon. Later the Persians conquered the Babylonians. King Xerxes (or Ahasuerus) reigned in Persia 486-465 B.C. Since Esther was a young woman when Xerxes was king, she must have been born—and orphaned—in the land of exile. She lived in Susa (in modern Iran near the border with Iraq). Her uncle Mordecai brought her up to know her people and her people's God. King Xerxes became angry with his queen and deposed her. In a nationwide coerced "beauty contest" he chose Esther as his new queen—not knowing she was Jewish. Then Haman, special adviser to Xerxes, furious that Mordecai would not bow to him, persuaded Xerxes to issue a decree that all Jews would be wiped out. *Read Esther 4:1—5:8.*

1. Identify the factors working for and against Esther in this passage.

2. When have you been faced with a situation so negative that you doubted you could wield any positive effect? What action did you take (or are you taking)?

3. What did Mordecai do in response to the king's edict (4:1-8)?

4. Why did Esther hesitate to get involved in the situation (4:9-11)?

5. When you are called on to approach someone and make a case for something important, what excuses are you tempted to offer?

6. How did Mordecai persuade Esther that she was the one to act (4:12-14)?

7. What steps did Esther take to prepare herself to approach the king (4:15-17)?

8. When the Lord calls you to take a risk, how do you enlist other people's support, both in prayers and in other ways? (Or if you don't get support, talk about why.)

9. Consider Esther's words, "And if I perish, I perish" (4:16). To what extent do you think such an attitude is necessary when God calls us to take a stand for something?

10. How did the king respond to Esther's unannounced appearance before the throne (5:1-3)?

11. If you are married, there has probably been a time when you have felt that you should talk to your spouse about something, but you were afraid to begin the conversation. Perhaps you feel that way now. Consider the example of how Esther approached Xerxes. (Her example applies to a husband approaching his wife as readily as to a wife approaching her husband.) What can you learn from Esther's strategy?

12. Esther did not immediately beg for the lives of her people. Instead she invited the king and Haman to a banquet. At the banquet, when the king again asked her what she wished, she invited the two of them to another banquet! How do you explain Esther's reserve (5:4-8)?

13. God honored Esther's prudence and courage. At the second banquet she made her appeal to the king, exposed Haman's treachery and saved her people (chapter 7). A married couple following God together can be a powerful influence on people and situations. Where might God be calling you as a couple to take a risk to influence others?

Or, if you are single, where might God be calling you to be an influence, and who might partner with you in that?

Pray for the courage to be an influence for good in your home and in your other areas of influence.

Now or Later

REFLECT: Mordecai asked Esther, "Who knows but that you have come to royal position for such a time as this?" Toward the bottom of a piece of paper, copy Mordecai's question, but leave the place for "royal position" blank: Who knows but that you have come to _____ for such a time as this?

Identify various "places" where the Lord has put you. Consider such factors as neighborhood, workplace, family connections, other relationships, stage of life, and degree of authority and responsibility. Fill in the blank with one place, and add others above the blank so you build a tower of your potential areas of influence. For example:

a management position at Morgan's Hardware
your mid-40s
the parents' organization at Newtown Middle School
Newtown Community Church
your friendship with Mary & John
the local library board
the bowling league
Who knows but that you have come to <u>the N. Elm St. neighborhood</u>
for such a time as this?

Prayerfully consider why God may have brought you to each of these places. Express your willingness for God to use you in each of these areas to draw people to himself.

READ Esther 7—8 from the king's perspective. In this study King Xerxes may seem to be the forgotten person. Discuss how, even though he was king, he was willing to be influenced by Esther.

FOR COUPLES. Do the first exercise under "Now or Later," but identify the places where God has put you *as a couple*. Pray about ways to serve him together. Serving together does not mean that you both do the same jobs but that your ministries complement each other. For example, if you want to use your home for ministry, you may do that in different ways but with the same aim.

Leader's Notes

MY GRACE IS SUFFICIENT FOR YOU. (2 COR 12:9)

Leading a Bible discussion can be an enjoyable and rewarding experience. But it can also be *scary*—especially if you've never done it before. If this is your feeling, you're in good company. When God asked Moses to lead the Israelites out of Egypt, he replied, "O Lord, please send someone else to do it!" (Ex 4:13). It was the same with Solomon, Jeremiah and Timothy, but God helped these people in spite of their weaknesses, and he will help you as well.

You don't need to be an expert on the Bible or a trained teacher to lead a Bible discussion. The idea behind these inductive studies is that the leader guides group members to discover for themselves what the Bible has to say. This method of learning will allow group members to remember much more of what is said than a lecture would.

These studies are designed to be led easily. As a matter of fact, the flow of questions through the passage from observation to interpretation to application is so natural that you may feel that the studies lead themselves. This study guide is also flexible. You can use it with a variety of groups— student, professional, neighborhood or church groups. Each study takes forty-five to sixty minutes in a group setting.

There are some important facts to know about group dynamics and encouraging discussion. The suggestions listed below should enable you to effectively and enjoyably fulfill your role as leader.

Preparing for the Study

1. Ask God to help you understand and apply the passage in your own life. Unless this happens, you will not be prepared to lead others. Pray too for the various members of the group. Ask God to open your hearts to the message of his Word and motivate you to action.

2. Read the introduction to the entire guide to get an overview of the entire book and the issues which will be explored.

3. As you begin each study, read and reread the assigned Bible passage to familiarize yourself with it.

4. This study guide is based on the New International Version of the Bible. It will help you and the group if you use this translation as the basis for your study and discussion.

5. Carefully work through each question in the study. Spend time in meditation and reflection as you consider how to respond.

6. Write your thoughts and responses in the space provided in the study guide. This will help you to express your understanding of the passage clearly.

7. It might help to have a Bible dictionary handy. Use it to look up any unfamiliar words, names or places. (For additional help on how to study a passage, see chapter five of *How to Lead a LifeGuide Bible Study,* InterVarsity Press.)

8. Consider how you can apply the Scripture to your life. Remember that the group will follow your lead in responding to the studies. They will not go any deeper than you do.

9. Once you have finished your own study of the passage, familiarize yourself with the leader's notes for the study you are leading. These are designed to help you in several ways. First, they tell you the purpose the study guide author had in mind when writing the study. Take time to think through how the study questions work together to accomplish that purpose. Second, the notes provide you with additional background information or suggestions on group dynamics for various questions. This information can be useful when people have difficulty understanding or answering a question. Third, the leader's notes can alert you to potential problems you may encounter during the study.

10. If you wish to remind yourself of anything mentioned in the leader's notes, make a note to yourself below that question in the study.

Leading the Study

1. Begin the study on time. Open with prayer, asking God to help the group to understand and apply the passage.

2. Be sure that everyone in your group has a study guide. Encourage the group to prepare beforehand for each discussion by reading the introduction to the guide and by working through the questions in the study.

3. At the beginning of your first time together, explain that these studies are meant to be discussions, not lectures. Encourage the members of the group to participate. However, do not put pressure on those who may be hesitant to speak during the first few sessions. You may want to suggest the following guidelines to your group.

☐ Stick to the topic being discussed.

☐ Your responses should be based on the verses which are the focus of the discussion and not on outside authorities such as commentaries or speakers.

☐ These studies focus on a particular passage of Scripture. Only rarely should you refer to other portions of the Bible. This allows for everyone to participate in in-depth study on equal ground.

☐ Anything said in the group is considered confidential and will not be discussed outside the group unless specific permission is given to do so.

☐ We will listen attentively to each other and provide time for each person present to talk.

☐ We will pray for each other.

4. Have a group member read the introduction at the beginning of the discussion.

5. Every session begins with a group discussion question. The question or activity is meant to be used before the passage is read. The question introduces the theme of the study and encourages group members to begin to open up. Encourage as many members as possible to participate, and be ready to get the discussion going with your own response.

This section is designed to reveal where our thoughts or feelings need to be transformed by Scripture. That is why it is especially important not to read the passage before the discussion question is asked. The passage will tend to color the honest reactions people would otherwise give because they are, of course, supposed to think the way the Bible does.

You may want to supplement the group discussion question with an icebreaker to help people to get comfortable. See the community section of *Small Group Idea Book* for more ideas.

You also might want to use the personal reflection question with your group. Either allow a time of silence for people to respond individually or discuss it together.

6. Have a group member (or members if the passage is long) read aloud the passage to be studied. Then give people several minutes to read the passage again silently so that they can take it all in.

7. Question 1 will generally be an overview question designed to briefly survey the passage. Encourage the group to look at the whole passage, but try to avoid getting sidetracked by questions or issues that will be addressed later in the study.

8. As you ask the questions, keep in mind that they are designed to be used just as they are written. You may simply read them aloud. Or you may prefer to express them in your own words.

There may be times when it is appropriate to deviate from the study guide.

For example, a question may have already been answered. If so, move on to the next question. Or someone may raise an important question not covered in the guide. Take time to discuss it, but try to keep the group from going off on tangents.

9. Avoid answering your own questions. If necessary, repeat or rephrase them until they are clearly understood. Or point out something you read in the leader's notes to clarify the context or meaning. An eager group quickly becomes passive and silent if they think the leader will do most of the talking.

10. Don't be afraid of silence. People may need time to think about the question before formulating their answers.

11. Don't be content with just one answer. Ask, "What do the rest of you think?" or "Anything else?" until several people have given answers to the question.

12. Acknowledge all contributions. Try to be affirming whenever possible. Never reject an answer. If it is clearly off-base, ask, "Which verse led you to that conclusion?" or again, "What do the rest of you think?"

13. Don't expect every answer to be addressed to you, even though this will probably happen at first. As group members become more at ease, they will begin to truly interact with each other. This is one sign of healthy discussion.

14. Don't be afraid of controversy. It can be very stimulating. If you don't resolve an issue completely, don't be frustrated. Move on and keep it in mind for later. A subsequent study may solve the problem.

15. Periodically summarize what the group has said about the passage. This helps to draw together the various ideas mentioned and gives continuity to the study. But don't preach.

16. At the end of the Bible discussion you may want to allow group members a time of quiet to work on an idea under "Now or Later." Then discuss what you experienced. Or you may want to encourage group members to work on these ideas between meetings. Give an opportunity during the session for people to talk about what they are learning.

17. Conclude your time together with conversational prayer, adapting the prayer suggestion at the end of the study to your group. Ask for God's help in following through on the commitments you've made.

18. End on time.

Many more suggestions and helps are found in *How to Lead a LifeGuide Bible Study.*

Components of Small Groups

A healthy small group should do more than study the Bible. There are four components to consider as you structure your time together.

Nurture. Small groups help us to grow in our knowledge and love of God. Bible study is the key to making this happen and is the foundation of your small group.

Community. Small groups are a great place to develop deep friendships with other Christians. Allow time for informal interaction before and after each study. Plan activities and games that will help you get to know each other. Spend time having fun together—going on a picnic or cooking dinner together.

Worship and prayer. Your study will be enhanced by spending time praising God together in prayer or song. Pray for each other's needs—and keep track of how God is answering prayer in your group. Ask God to help you to apply what you are learning in your study.

Outreach. Reaching out to others can be a practical way of applying what you are learning, and it will keep your group from becoming self-focused. Host a series of evangelistic discussions for your friends or neighbors. Clean up the yard of an elderly friend. Serve at a soup kitchen together, or spend a day working on a Habitat house.

Many more suggestions and helps in each of these areas are found in *Small Group Idea Book.* Information on building a small group can be found in *Small Group Leaders' Handbook* and *The Big Book on Small Groups* (both from Inter-Varsity Press). Reading through one of these books would be worth your time.

Study 1. Adam and Eve: Ideal Companions. Genesis 2:15—3:13.

Purpose: To appreciate God's ideal for marriage and to understand how sin warps even the best relationships.

Question 2. "The word *Eden* refers to a well-watered place, suggesting a luxuriant park. The word translated 'garden' does not typically refer to vegetable plots but to orchards or parks containing trees" (John H. Walton, Victor H. Matthews and Mark W. Chavalas, *The IVP Bible Background Commentary: Old Testament* [Downers Grove, Ill.: InterVarsity Press, 2000], p. 31).

The man's life in Eden was not entirely one of leisure. He had the responsibility to work the garden and take care of it. Work was part of the man's life even before the fall. He could eat the fruit of any tree except one, the tree of the knowledge of good and evil; that prohibition appears to be the only specific moral rule God gave him.

Question 3. When God says the man is "alone," he does not mean merely that the man is unmarried. At this point the man is the *only* human being on earth. He lacks human companionship of any sort: marriage, family, friends, even casual acquaintances. Even while human nature was still unaffected by sin, the first human being had an unfulfilled need for companionship of his own kind. The fact that the man needed something, even in Eden, is not inconsistent with Eden's perfection. The man also needed food and meaningful work (2:15-16).

Question 5. "In order to teach the close connection that woman has with man, the text does not say that God also created her from 'the ground' or 'the dust of the ground'; instead, she came from one of Adam's ribs. Thus the phrase 'bone of my bones and flesh of my flesh' pointed not only to the woman's origin, but also to the closeness of her marriage relationship and the partnership she was to share with her mate.

"It is not without significance that the Hebrew word for 'rib' appears nowhere else with this meaning in the Hebrew Bible; its usual meaning is 'side.' Thus, as some of the Reformers put it, woman was not taken from man's feet, as if she were beneath him, or from his head, as if she were over him, but from his side, as an equal with him. . . . The point is that man and woman together share a commonality and partnership observed nowhere else in the created order. To emphasize this closeness, God actually took a real part from the side of the man as he brought to life for the first time this new creation called woman" (Walter C. Kaiser Jr., et al., *Hard Sayings of the Bible* [Downers Grove, Ill.: InterVarsity Press, 1996], p. 95).

Contrary to a once-popular myth, men do *not* have one fewer rib than women!

Question 6. Although the name "Eve" does not appear until Genesis 3:20, it is simpler to refer to the first woman as Eve.

Question 7. A possible follow-up or alternate question: "Because Adam and Eve fell, sin entered the world. Even the best marriages are now marred by sin. If a perfect marriage is now impossible, what value is there in knowing God's ideal for marriage?"

Question 8. Some suggest that the serpent planted doubt that God had actually spoken. The serpent was even more devious: he acknowledged that God had spoken, but he misquoted God and expanded the prohibition from one tree to *all* the trees in the garden (3:1). He denied that Adam and Eve would die (3:4) and promised them godlike power and knowledge (3:5). The fruit's threefold appeal (3:6) has a parallel in 1 John 2:16: "the cravings of sinful man, the lust of his eyes and the boasting of what he has and does," or as the KJV expresses it, "the lust of the flesh, and the lust of the eyes, and the pride of life."

Question 10. Sin did not end the first couple's relationship with their Creator or with each other, but it destroyed their free intimacy. After Adam and Eve covered themselves in shame and tried to hide from God, they resorted to accusations. The man blamed both God and the woman; the woman blamed the serpent. At least both were honest enough to admit that they had eaten from the tree. Even when they ran from God, God in his mercy pursued them, confronted them and continued to communicate with them.

Now or Later. Each one of these sections has an exercise just for couples. If you are studying in a group, you can use these in one of two ways: (1) allow five to ten minutes at the end of your study for couples to do these together, and then come back together for closing prayer; or (2) encourage couples to do these between small group meetings.

Study 2. Abraham and Sarah: Waiting Together. Genesis 17:1-8, 15-22; 21:1-7.

Purpose: To submit to God the times of waiting in our marriages and in our individual lives.

Questions 1-2. "Failure to produce an heir was a major calamity for a family in the ancient world because it meant a disruption in the generational inheritance pattern and left no one to care for the couple in their old age" (*IVP Bible Background Commentary: Old Testament*, p. 43).

Question 3. Four new names appear in this passage. God pronounces a new name for himself: "El Shaddai," or "God Almighty," which is the first time this name for God occurs in Scripture (17:1). God changes the name of Abram (exalted father) to Abraham (father of many) (17:5). There is no clear alteration of meaning when he changes Sarai's name to Sarah (17:15), since both evidently mean "princess." After Abraham falls down laughing, God says that the son to be born to Abraham and Sarah will be named Isaac, or "he laughs" (17:19).

"Names had power in the ancient world. By naming the animals, Adam demonstrated his mastery over them. In a similar way, God's changing Abram's name to Abraham and Sarai's name to Sarah signifies both a reiteration of the covenant promise and the designation of these people as God's chosen servants" (*IVP Bible Background Commentary: Old Testament*, p. 49).

Question 5. Possible follow-up question: When have you become impatient with God's timing and forged ahead with your own solution to a problem? With what outcome?

Question 6. God assured Abraham that Ishmael (ancestor of the Arab peoples) would be blessed and would become a great nation; but God's covenant would be with Isaac, the son of Sarah and Abraham. God called the couple to continue to wait for him and to refrain from their own schemes. At this point

God became very specific about timing. Isaac would be born "by this time next year" (17:21).

Your group no doubt includes couples and individuals who are waiting on God: perhaps for children, for guidance in a move, for material provision, for a legal question to be settled, for employment. They probably do not have the benefit—which Abraham and Sarah had—of a specific, definite verbal promise from God. They may need even more faith than was asked of Sarah and Abraham because they have no specific answer to watch for.

Question 7. If it is appropriate, personalize this question for couples in your group: "How have you helped and encouraged each other to wait for God?"

Question 8. It is possible to make good on a promise simply because we have a contract, with no emotional involvement. But the Lord "was gracious to Sarah as he had said." His fulfillment was a kind and generous gift to her. God also arranged Isaac's birth "at the very time God had promised." God's fulfillment was not random but was specific in its timing.

Question 9. Abraham did not accept God's gift and then casually forget him. We see two acts of obedience on Abraham's part: he named his son Isaac as God had commanded (17:19), and he circumcised him as a sign of the covenant (see 17:9-14).

Question 10. Abraham laughed at the seeming absurdity of an idea; Sarah laughed in amazed joy when it came true. In fairness we must add that Sarah laughed in disbelief when she overheard one of three men—likely the Lord himself—say she would have a son (18:10-15).

Study 3. Isaac and Rebekah: How God Makes a Match. Genesis 24:26-67.
Purpose: To trust God's wisdom in the choice of a marriage partner.

Question 2. The following notes will be helpful to more fully explain the servant's mission to find a wife for Isaac:

"Two matters are of primary importance to Abraham: that the girl be from his own kindred (24:4), and that she be willing to come to Canaan (vss. 4-9, 38-41, 54-58). By the first, Abraham sought to guard Isaac, his son of promise, from the seduction of the heathen, Canaanite religion. . . . By the second, Abraham guarded his son from the necessity or temptation of leaving the Promised Land; for it is in 'this land' (12:7; 15:7, 18; 24:7) that Yahweh would make Abraham a great nation. Here at the end of his life Abraham showed himself faithful to his call by maintaining the integrity of these two elements—land and seed" (R. Lansing Hicks, in *Interpreter's Dictionary of the Bible*, vol. 1, ed. George A. Buttrick [Nashville, Tenn.: Abingdon Press, 1962], p. 18).

"There must have been a very great inducement to Abraham to marry his son to one of the local chieftains, thus making an alliance with one of them, and also gaining a footing in the land; but his obedience and faith shine out with splendour" (E. F. Kevan, in *The New Bible Commentary,* ed. F. Davidson [Grand Rapids, Mich.: Eerdmans, 1965], pp. 29-30).

Question 7. "It was unusual in the ancient world for the woman to have any part in major decisions. Rebekah was not consulted with regard to the marriage (vv. 50-51), but when the servant asked to leave right away the men looked to Rebekah for consent. Marriage contracts of this general period show a great concern for maintaining the woman's security within her husband's family. The presence of her family was one of the guarantees that she would be cared for and treated properly. The ten days that Rebekah's family requested (v. 55) would have given them a little more opportunity to make sure that everything was as it appeared to be. It is likely that she was consulted because of the substantial risk that was involved in leaving the family protection under such unusual circumstances" (*IVP Bible Background Commentary: Old Testament,* p. 56).

Question 9. Isaac waited and remained watchful. We sense that he had gone out into the field to watch for the returning caravan (v. 63). He could not know whether the servant had been successful and would return with the wife whom God had chosen. When Isaac heard the story (v. 66), he had no question about Rebekah but married her immediately. Even today in some cultures the bride and groom do not meet until their wedding day. Such an arrangement takes trust in the wisdom of those who have arranged the marriage. In the case of Isaac and Rebekah, the servant's story made it clear that a sovereign and loving God had brought the two together.

Study 4. Jacob and Rachel: Love Endures. Genesis 29:1-30.

Purpose: To maintain hope that the Lord knows and will meet all our needs.

Question 2. Concerning the stone over the well (v. 2): "The stone served a double function, as a guard against contamination or poisoning of the well and as a social control mechanism, preventing any of the herdsmen in the area from drawing more water than was their right. . . . The stone may even have served to disguise the location of the well from the casual passerby. Wells of this time were not surrounded by protective walls, so the stone would also have prevented animals (or people) from inadvertently stumbling into it" (*IVP Bible Background Commentary: Old Testament,* p. 61).

Concerning Rachel's tending her father's sheep (v. 9): "While it is not uncommon today for women and small children to herd Bedouin flocks, in antiquity women would have done so only when the household had no sons. It was a dangerous practice since they might be molested, but it was also a way of attracting a husband" (*IVP Bible Background Commentary: Old Testament*, p. 61).

Concerning Jacob's kiss (v. 11): "The traditional form of greeting for friends and relatives in the Middle East is a warm hug and a kiss on each cheek. This was done with both male and female relatives" (*IVP Bible Background Commentary: Old Testament*, p. 61).

Question 6. "Jacob, who had overreached his brother and deceived his old father, is now deceived himself. In this deception, Laban takes advantage of the fact that the bride was brought to her husband veiled" (*New Bible Commentary*, p. 97).

Questions 7-8. Jacob could have left with Leah, but he did not love her and would have had to leave Rachel behind. He could have abandoned Leah and fled from the situation, but Laban would have hunted him down, and his brother Esau was already after him! He chose to stay with the woman he loved and bind himself to the trickster Laban for seven more years. Even in this warped situation, the God-given love of a man and woman prevailed.

Note that Jacob did not have to serve Laban seven more years before he could marry Rachel. He had to wait only a week before he took her as his second wife, but then he had to stay around and serve Laban seven more years. The seven-day marriage celebration appears to be customary; see Judges 14:10-12.

Jacob's marriage to two women caused numerous problems later, as polygamy does throughout the Bible. His brother Esau had already married multiple wives (Gen 26:34-35; 28:8-9). "Polygamy was never lawful for any of the persons in the Bible. There never existed any express biblical permission for such a deviation from the ordinance of God made at the institution of marriage in the Garden of Eden (Gen 2:21-24). . . . Scripture does not always pause to state the obvious. In many cases there is no need for the reader to imagine what God thinks of such states of affairs, for the misfortune and strife that come into the domestic lives of these polygamists cannot be read as a sign of divine approval" (*Hard Sayings*, p. 130).

Study 5. Boaz and Ruth: Faithfulness Rewarded. Ruth 2:1-13; 4:1-17.
Purpose: To understand that God blesses a marriage when the partners are faithful to him and to each other.
Group discussion. If there are singles in your group, encourage them to think about brothers- and sisters-in-law.

Question 2. Gleaning was one of God's provisions for the poor and the foreigner in the land (Lev 19:9-10; Deut 24:19-22). Ruth took the initiative to go out and gather food for herself and Naomi. It was a somewhat risky position for a woman to put herself in (2:9). Although Naomi knew about Boaz, there is no indication that Ruth deliberately went to Boaz's field. Ruth 2:3 says, "As it turned out" she went there; but as the Lord was choosing the ancestors for David and ultimately for Jesus, Ruth's destination could not have been accidental.

Question 3. Another way to put it is: How do you discern whether a person is trying too desperately to find a partner without trusting God or too passively waiting on God without making any effort to meet people?

Question 8. "The kinsman-redeemer's role was to help recover the tribe's losses, whether those losses were human (in which case he hunted down the killer), judicial (in which case he assisted in lawsuits) or economic (in which case he recovered the property of a family member). Since Yahweh had granted the land to the Israelites as tenants, they could not sell it, and if they mortgaged a portion of it to pay debts, it was considered very important to regain ownership as soon as possible. In this way the land remained within the extended family as a sign of its membership in the covenantal community. . . . The benefits that derived from functioning as a kinsman-redeemer required that a sequence of priorities be established. Closer relatives were therefore given the opportunity to exercise that function first" (*IVP Bible Background Commentary: Old Testament*, pp. 279-80).

Question 9. Boaz gives the other kinsman a fair chance to redeem the land and to claim Ruth, although Boaz clearly hopes that the kinsman will turn down the opportunity! "Once Boaz interprets the kinsman responsibilities as including marrying Ruth, the economic picture changes considerably. . . . If the kinsman must marry Ruth, the son that may be born to her would then be the heir to the property of Elimelech's family. In this case the money that is used to redeem the land is not an investment but simply reduces his family assets. . . . It is even possible that Ruth's children would have a claim to a portion of his inheritance along with any children he already had. It is likely he is married; the economic impact on his family of redeeming Ruth is thus a chief criterion in his decision" (*IVP Bible Background Commentary: Old Testament*, p. 280).

Question 11. An alternative way to ask this question would be: How is your marriage (or your life) better because you have tried to consistently obey the Lord? Perhaps the greatest blessing of obedience is the inner certainty that our lives are pleasing to him. We can look for more tangible rewards in this life, but we should not demand a certain degree of material blessings or status for our obedience.

Study 6. Elkanah and Hannah: Dealing with Disappointment. 1 Samuel 1.
Purpose: To equip marriage partners, and Christians in general, to encourage each other in the face of disappointment.
Question 3. "Polygamy, at variance with the ideal of marriage (Gen 2:24), was practiced by Abram, Jacob, Gideon, David, and Solomon. This bigamous marriage (probably in accord with Deut 21:15-17), was undoubtedly caused by a childless first marriage. No moral blame is here attached to Elkanah's marriages" (Fred E. Young, in *The Wycliffe Bible Commentary,* ed. Charles F. Pfeiffer and Everett F. Harrison [Nashville, Tenn.: The Southwestern Co., 1962], p. 274).
Question 4. "Since bearing children was a sign of God's greatest blessing (Ps 127:3), the inability to bear children was often viewed as a sign of God's punishment. Additionally, a woman's status in the family would be very tenuous if she had not borne children. A barren woman could be and often was discarded, ostracized or given a lower status" (*IVP Bible Background Commentary: Old Testament,* p. 281).
Question 6. "Silent prayer did not characterize early Hebrew praying. Hannah's unusual type of prayer caused Eli to think her drunk" (*Wycliffe Commentary,* p. 275).

Hannah's vow in verse 11 may appear that she was making a deal with God: you do this for me, and I'll do this for you. In reality she was carrying out a common practice in ancient Near Eastern cultures: to make a request of God with a vow to offer a sacrifice or gift in gratitude when God answered favorably.

With her promise that no razor would ever touch her son's head, Hannah was vowing that her son would be set apart for the Lord as a Nazirite. The specifics of this special covenant are spelled out in Numbers 6:1-21. Although the Scriptural separation was temporary (see Num 6:13), Hannah vowed to give her son to the Lord for his entire life (v. 11). The Lord set apart Samson as a Nazirite even before he was conceived (Judg 13:5).
Question 7. Hannah took courage because Eli expressed a wish that God would answer her. Her actions say that she took his words as a promise from God that her prayers would be answered. Perhaps there was something in his presence and character that simply reassured her. We should thank God for people whose simple words of encouragement can turn us from dejection to hope.

Study 7. David and Abigail: Wise Intervention. 1 Samuel 25:14-42.

Purpose: To become more aware of God's intervention in our lives through wise people.

Question 3. David had ordered four hundred of his men to put on their swords and accompany him (v. 13). From verses 21-22 we can have no doubt about David's plans. He intended to kill every male in Nabal's household. Nabal's servant was right when he reported to Abigail that "disaster is hanging over our master and his whole household" (v. 17).

Question 4. Abigail recognized the urgency of the situation. She "lost no time" (v. 18). "Nabal had listed bread, water and meat as rewards for his servants (25:11), and now Abigail includes two hundred loaves, two skins of wine and five butchered sheep as part of her gift. This acknowledges the service David and his men had done in protecting Nabal's herds. . . . [The further items] were stored food items and would serve David's company well" (*IVP Bible Background Commentary: Old Testament*, p. 316). Abigail kept her action secret from Nabal (v. 19). Secrecy between husband and wife is usually unhealthy, but in this case Abigail's secrecy was designed to save Nabal's life. Had he known of her plans, he would have put a stop to them and sealed his own doom.

Question 5. In her appeal to David, Abigail managed to be both humble and shrewd. She freely agreed that Nabal was wrong (v. 25), asked David to forgive him (v. 28), assumed that David would *not* carry through with his plans for revenge (v. 26), expressed confidence that God would protect David and make him great (vv. 28-30), reminded David that as king he would not want a guilty conscience (v. 31) and asked him to remember her favorably when he became leader of Israel (v. 31). As for her donkey train of gifts (v. 18), she mentioned it only in passing (v. 27).

"Abigail managed to stop an army in its tracks, armed only with tact and charm, and with a demonstration of deep humility. . . . [S]he protected David's dignity by scarcely mentioning the provisions he and his men needed so desperately, almost as if she'd cooked up a little basket for afternoon tea. She forwent her privileged status as Nabal's wife and humbled herself completely before David. There is nothing as powerful to bring about a change of heart as the presence of humility and meekness in the face of prideful anger" (Rebecca Manley Pippert, *A Heart for God* [Downers Grove, Ill.: InterVarsity Press, 2002], p. 183).

Question 8. David praised the Lord and pronounced a blessing on Abigail. With no suggestion of reluctance, he let go of his plans for revenge. We can almost hear him sigh with relief that God sent someone to intervene to stop him from vengeful killing.

Study 8. Hosea and Gomer: Unconditional Love. Hosea 1 and 3.

Purpose: To forgive others through the power and love of God.

Question 1. "The contents of the book are a mirror of the political, social and religious conditions prevailing in Israel in the days of the prophet. The last decades of the life of the northern kingdom were marked by a frantic and senseless change of policies—now courting the favour of Assyria, now trying to bribe Egypt. Instead of putting their trust in their God, the leaders of the nation tried to save the country by means of political schemes which, by the very nature of things, were destined to lead to disaster.

"The religious leaders of the people proved themselves to be equally unworthy. The form of religion prevailing in Hosea's day was an amalgam of the worship of Jehovah and the idolatrous religion of Canaan" (*New Bible Commentary*, p. 682).

Question 3. God sometimes called his prophets to do unconventional things, and the marriage of Hosea to Gomer ranks as one of the most unusual prophetic acts in Scripture. The marriage was ordained by God as a flesh-and-blood illustration of Israel's spiritual unfaithfulness and the Lord's loving reconciliation with his people (v. 2). It was a one-of-a-kind coupling to proclaim a message for that time and place.

In some Bible translations, God tells Hosea to take a "wife of harlotry" (RSV, NASB) or "wife of whoredoms" (KJV). By contrast "an adulterous wife" (NIV) is mild, but the practical implications are the same: Hosea's wife would pursue other men and would be chronically unfaithful. How could God tell his prophet to contract such a marriage? Some interpreters hold that Gomer was pure when Hosea married her, but the Lord knew she was bent toward promiscuity. In any case God's reasons are plainly stated: the marriage will be a picture of Israel's idolatry and God's faithfulness.

Question 4. The names of the children may be shocking to your group members. It doesn't fit the way that we name our children today, but there are other uncomplimentary names in the Bible (for example, Ichabod in 1 Sam 4:21; Ben-Oni in Gen 35:18; Mara in Ruth 1:20).

The name Jezreel (vv. 4-5) refers to the slaughter of the remnants of the family and supporters of Ahab, a particularly wicked king of Israel (2 Kings 10). The Lord's statement, "I will put an end to the kingdom of Israel," was fulfilled in 721 B.C. when the Assyrians conquered Samaria, the capital of Israel, and took the people into exile. The southern kingdom of Judah endured longer.

Question 9. The marriage of Hosea and Gomer was a very unusual situation ordained by God to symbolize spiritual truths. This session deals with forgiveness between husbands and wives and between people in general. However, it is not within the scope of this study to try to answer all questions about marital infidelity, how to deal with it, or whether or when to reconcile with an unfaithful spouse.

Question 10. "Given the value of the barley added to the fifteen shekels of silver, one estimate would make Hosea's total outlay approximately thirty shekels. This amount is equal to the amount due as compensation for the loss of a slave in Exodus 21:32. Since Gomer's situation is unclear, it is not possible to make a definite determination of why Hosea would pay out this amount. Based on Middle Assyrian Law, however, he may be redeeming her from a legal situation from which she could not extricate herself (such as paying a debt she owed)" (*IVP Bible Background Commentary: Old Testament*, p. 753).

Study 9. King Xerxes and Esther: Courageous Influence. Esther 4:1—5:8.
Purpose: To see our spheres of influence as opportunities for the Lord and to resolve to use them to influence others for good.

Question 3. Mordecai was convinced that because of the king's regard for her, Esther was the Jewish people's best hope. He was both insistent and persistent. He gave Esther's servant Hathach detailed information about the threat and a copy of the edict for Hathach to explain to Esther, and he told Hathach to urge Esther to go to the king. We sense his urgency in every move. He wanted to leave Esther no room to sidestep this opportunity to act.

Question 4. "Whereas one might think that the queen and chief wife of the king would have many opportunities to have a passing word with the king, such was not necessarily the case. The queen did not regularly share the king's bed, nor were their meals taken together. She had her own private quarters. While she could be invited to join the king in the audience chamber, she did not have unlimited access" (*IVP Bible Background Commentary: Old Testament*, p. 488).

Question 6. Mordecai's words reveal his faith in God's power and sovereignty. After spending much effort to convince Esther that she is *the* person to go to the king, Mordecai stated in so many words that God could find another way ("relief and deliverance for the Jews will arise from another place"), but Esther and her family would miss out on the deliverance. Though he put it in the form of a question ("who knows but that you have come . . . for such a time as this?") his question is actually an expression of confidence that God had put Esther where she was for a specific purpose.

Question 7. Esther committed herself to fast for three days. She enlisted the support of her servants (who may not have been Jewish) and "all the Jews in

Susa" to join her in the fast. "In the Old Testament the religious use of fasting is often in connection with making a request before God. The principle is that the importance of the request causes an individual to be so concerned about their spiritual condition that physical necessities fade into the background. In this sense the act of fasting is designed as a process leading to purification and humbling oneself before God (Ps 69:10)" (*IVP Bible Background Commentary: Old Testament*, p. 488).

Question 9. "There is an abandonment about Esther's statement, but not the abandonment of resignation or despair. She placed in God's hands not only her appeal to the king, but her own physical life. While Esther did not wish for her own death, she valued obedience to God more highly than preserving her life. She would go to the king and try to save her people, and she would leave to God what happened to her personally. Her faith was in God rather than in the king or in her ability to persuade him" (Sandy Larsen, *A Woman of Grace* [Downers Grove, Ill.: InterVarsity Press, 1997], p. 61).

Question 11. Most couples will be very familiar with the need to talk and the fear of talking. They may not fear death, and they probably don't look for a golden scepter; but they do think twice before they bring up the touchy subject, and they watch for any sign of favor or disfavor. Couples can commit themselves to take Esther's example as a model for how to wisely influence each other for good.

Dale and Sandy Larsen are freelance writers living in Greenville, Illinois. They have authored over thirty Bible study guides, including the LifeGuide® Bible Studies Hosea: God's Persistent Love *and* Faith: Depending on God.

What Should We Study Next?

A good place to continue your study of Scripture would be with a book study. Many groups begin with a Gospel such as *Mark* (20 studies by Jim Hoover) or *John* (26 studies by Douglas Connelly). These guides are divided into two parts so that if twenty or twenty-six weeks seems like too much to do at once, the group can feel free to do half and take a break with another topic. Later you might want to come back to it. You might prefer to try a shorter letter. *Philippians* (9 studies by Donald Baker), *Ephesians* (11 studies by Andrew T. and Phyllis J. Le Peau) and *1 & 2 Timothy and Titus* (11 studies by Pete Sommer) are good options. If you want to vary your reading with an Old Testament book, consider *Ecclesiastes* (12 studies by Bill and Teresa Syrios) for a challenging and exciting study.

There are a number of interesting topical LifeGuide studies as well. Here are some options for filling three or four quarters of a year:

Basic Discipleship
Christian Beliefs, 12 studies by Stephen D. Eyre
Christian Character, 12 studies by Andrea Sterk & Peter Scazzero
Christian Disciplines, 12 studies by Andrea Sterk & Peter Scazzero
Evangelism, 12 studies by Rebecca Pippert & Ruth Siemens

Building Community
Fruit of the Spirit, 9 studies by Hazel Offner
Spiritual Gifts, 12 studies by Charles & Anne Hummel
Christian Community, 10 studies by Rob Suggs

Character Studies
David, 12 studies by Jack Kuhatschek
New Testament Characters, 10 studies by Carolyn Nystrom
Old Testament Characters, 12 studies by Peter Scazzero
Women of the Old Testament, 12 studies by Gladys Hunt

The Trinity
Meeting God, 12 studies by J. I. Packer
Meeting Jesus, 13 studies by Leighton Ford
Meeting the Spirit, 10 studies by Douglas Connelly